25 Reasons to Live. There is Always Hope!

BOB MILES

BOB MILES

ISBN: 1482669447
ISBN-13: 9781482669442

DEDICATION

This book is dedicated to all those people that have lost hope and their way in this world. Those special, beautiful people gave up all too soon. This book is also dedicated to all of those special people that have touched my life and ended theirs before I had a chance to say how much they were truly loved and very much needed.

Also, a dedication goes to all those that have make a choice to live through their pain and sorrow. You have made the correct choice. Congratulations and God Bless you.

BOB MILES

CONTENTS

ACKNOWLEDGMENTS

I would like to acknowledge my wonderful wife, Janet, who inspires me every day through her actions and loving kindness. Janet is a wonderful wife to me and mother to our two children Lily and Chloe.

I would also like to acknowledge Mary Hill for her inspiration in writing this book.

Again and again, I need to acknowledge the Father, Son and Holy Spirit for guiding me every second of my life.

As always, I wish to recognize the rosary and Jesus prayers that brings blessing into my life.

INTRODUCTION

Long ago and far away, I had the unexpected experience to work at the William Rowen Grant Funeral Home in Southampton, Pennsylvania. Mr. Grant was a neighbor and had a part time job opening. In the summers during high school, I would work full-time for him doing odd jobs around the funeral home. During college, I worked on the weekends picking up deceased bodies from their homes and helping out with viewings and funerals.

During this period, I was able to see many people I knew come in with their family members and friends to view the wake of the deceased. The majority of the deceased passed on naturally of old age or an unexpected illness. However, there were the funerals for the ones that every so often ended their lives prematurely. In plain words, they committed suicide.

For these viewings and funerals, I noticed that they were almost never found in the obituary columns of the newspaper. I suspect that they were intentionally not advertised. I can only guess that the family of the suicide victim just did not want the world to know the truth of how the departed left this world. Also, the viewings had an atmosphere of heavy somberness, notably more than the typical viewing. There was always an eerie silence in the room. At a typical viewing, people gathered in small groups and talked among themselves and you may have even heard some laughter as someone recalled a light hearted story about the deceased.

Suicide viewings had a sense of disbelief that the body lying in the coffin could have left so much behind in their wake. Many had left spouses, children, parents, friends, teachers and people who loved them very dearly standing in disbelief that this person could have done such a thing. What led to this? Could someone have prevented this? Did they have something to do with them ending their life? Why didn't they do something to prevent this? These are some of the questions that go unanswered.

Did the person who took their own life know that they are loved…that they are needed? They are fearfully and wonderfully made and that everything in the natural world is only temporary at best. Did they know that in the next minute anything can change for the better?

Another duty I had while working at the funeral home was to drive their one black limousine for weddings and rock concerts that came to the Philadelphia area. I remember one summer afternoon driving for the Bob

Welch group. Bob was the former singer/songwriter for the Fleetwood Mac group. Bob and I spent the day together and into the evening. He seemed like such an affable guy with the world on a string. On June 7, 2012, Bob committed suicide in Nashville, Tennessee. Bob had suffered from a spinal illness and feared that he would leave his wife to care for him on a full-time basis. He did not want this for her and decided to end his life.

I have known many people in my life that had ended their own lives all too soon. They decided that this world was too much to deal with and disappointment after disappointment kept creeping into their life. They lost hope. They lost all hope and could not see past their despair. If they only knew that there is hope and that life is not always about getting your own way, but to do God's will. It is not the will of God for you to control your destiny. It never was in your control anyway.

I hope this book gives you hope that there is always a better future if you give up control and let God control your life. No matter what you are facing, give up the control but do not give up on God. God can and will change things for the better. By having both faith and belief that God has a plan for you, you will see things differently. You will still be here to see the brighter and better future that is right in front of you.

FORWARD

Bob Miles has done it again. He has touched our hearts, as only he can. This time he approaches a difficult subject and he shows us how to deal with it.

Did you know that the suicide rate in the US in 2012 was 0.1 in 1,000. That is a lot of lost souls that could have done great things for humanity or changed history.

I have had the sad experience of losing a friend, by them ending their life. I have seen the scars it leaves on those left behind. The lasting questions, finality, grief, loss, lack of understanding, feeling unloved, lack of self love, the sense of guilt. This is the legacy a suicide leaves.

If you know of someone who is depressed, and has thoughts of suicide – PLEASE have them read this book. It has answers and alternatives to help and encourage them. Everyone should read this book, it will lift your spirit.

Kudos to you Bob, and thank you for caring.

Mary Hill,
Published Author

1

THERE IS ALWAYS HOPE

Please believe. Always believe that things can and will change and that there is hope for a new beginning. Should you be suffering with cancer or be imprisoned, there is always hope. I watched a television show called "The Incurables". The episode that I watched was about a teenage girl with stage 4 cancer and there was apparently no hope.

However, the father of the girl knew better and knew that there was hope. Her father constantly used the internet to research her cancer and discovered a holistic doctor who combined his treatments with her primary care medical doctor. After just four weeks, the girl with stage 4 cancer was cancer-free.

For those imprisoned, Nelson Mandela, former president of South Africa spent 27 years in prison. After his release, in 1993, he won the Nobel Peace Prize.

There is always hope in any situation. You have to set your mind that you will never give up. You will win and nothing is ever hopeless. It is when you quit and give up that hope fades away. Never give up! Never give up! Never give up! Never give up! Never give up! Never give up!

There is always hope.

Psalm 42:11
New King James Version (NKJV) 11
[11] Why are you cast down, O my soul?
And why are you disquieted within me?
Hope in God;
For I shall yet praise Him,
The help of my countenance and my God.

2

TOMORROW IS A NEW DAY

Every day is new and every time we wake up it is a new beginning. The past is gone. In the movie, "Kung-Fu Panda", there is a famous quote that the turtle delivers to the panda. The turtle tells the panda bear, "Yesterday is history, tomorrow is a mystery, Today? Today is a gift. That is why we call it the present." Today and right now is truly a present. No matter how much we mess up today, we have tomorrow to start over. This is called a do-over.

In the film, "City Slickers", Billy Crystal's character says to his friend who is facing the fact that he is turning 40 years old, that his friend's life is a do-over. You can and always have the gift of a do-over. You can go back and apologize to someone that you have hurt, or you can change any situation for the better.

Let us say that at one time in your life you stole from a store or worse, you robbed a bank. You can always start new with a clean slate. Once you have paid your debt to the laws of your society, then your past is gone and it is time for a do-over.

On a side note, I would have said to the character in City Slickers, that it is a gift to turn 40 years old.......many people are not given the gift to grow old, so do not complain!

As for the people who try to remind you of your past, politely know that when they point a finger at you, there are three fingers on their hand that points back to them.

---

2 Corinthians 5:17
New King James Version (NKJV) 17
[17] Therefore, if anyone is in Christ, he is a new creation; old things have passed away; behold, all thing have become new.

3

YOU CAN CONTROL YOUR THOUGHTS

Our minds can be a mess. We can live in an isolated world of phobias that only exist in our thoughts. Usually late in the evening or in the wee hours of the morning, the negative thoughts seep in like gas into a chamber to suffocate our true identity of who we can become.

Anytime we are alone, we suffer in our thoughts. It is amazing how often we can think negative thoughts throughout the day. It is said that the average person has over 60,000 thoughts per day and over 80% of these thoughts are negative.

You need to have a plan of action that works for you. I have learned to program myself to say a rotation of prayers that take the place of such destructive thoughts. I often pray the rosary or the Jesus prayer. When I find that I am thinking negatively, I quickly switch my thought pattern and say these prayers over and over again. I refuse to let past events into my mind. However, do not get discouraged if once in a while they do slip in.

You can always find a prayer that works best for you. A group of words that bring peace into your life is your goal. You have to say these words repeatedly to yourself to drown out the negativity that our subconscious mind creates. This truly works every time.

Genesis 6:5
New King James Version (NKJV) 5
5 Then the Lord saw that the wickedness of man was great in the earth, and that every intent of the thoughts of his heart was only evil continually.

4

MIRACLES DO HAPPEN AND WILL HAPPEN TO YOU

Sometimes all we need is a miracle. Those that have had miracles happen to them never thought it would but it did. Kathryn Kuhlman had a television show in the 1960s and 1970s called, "I believe in Miracles." On this show were regular people that had testimony after testimony of miracles that happened in their daily lives. There were shows where people were cured of incurable cancers to bones growing in sockets where there were no bones.

Today, Sid Roth has a great television show called, "It's Supernatural." On Roth's show, there are current day miracles similar to those that have happened on Kathryn Kulman's show. In chapter one, I spoke about another great show called, "The Incurables." This show features those that have incurable diseases that end up being cured.

There certainly is strong evidence of miracles taking place every day. Please check out these shows on the internet such as YouTube or on television. They will bring you hope. You can have a miracle take place in your life if you have hope. Nothing is impossible.

I read where we all at some point or another have cancer in our bodies and do not ever know it. That cancer goes away over time and we are cured without having any knowledge of our illness. I would call this a miracle.

New King James Version (NKJV) 6
[6] And the multitudes with one accord heeded the things spoken by Phillip, hearing and seeing the miracles which he did.

5

LOOK FROM ABOVE AND NOT BELOW

When you look up at your problem, it can be very big and daunting. However, when you look down at your problem, then it does not seem so big.

I remember a comedian on television who would put the image of someone in between their index finger and thumb and then squeeze them together while imagining that they were making the person tiny. You can do this as well with your problems.

The more you attach yourself to your problem, the more pain you attach to yourself. You have to distance yourself from your problem. Think of your problem as being behind you by a hundred years. What would it matter today if we did something a hundred or so years ago? In the reverse, what will our problem look like in a hundred years from today? Not too much, I would say. The problem will be all but forgotten and very small.

This is how you have to look at your problems today, as if they were so small that in time it would not have ever mattered. Look down on your situation and it will look small. This is how you push through and move forward. Look from above and not below.

Genesis 28:13
New King James Version (NKJV)
13 And behold, the Lord stood above it and said, "I *am* the Lord God of Abraham your father and the God of Isaac; the land on which you lie I will give to you and your descendants.

6

LIVE IN THE PRESENT

This is a Big One! Did you know that at this very moment you have no problems? You are reading this book, breathing, functioning and there are no problems at all. It is when you think about your problems and your situation that you have a problem. However, as you sit at this very minute, you really have no problems.

As I write this, I have no problems whatsoever. Should I have stage 4 cancer and I am diagnosed to die soon, I have no problems at this very moment. So live in this very moment and problems do not exist. This is why living for now is what so many of the great sages, philosophers, prophets and saints have spoken about throughout the centuries.

Learn from those that have passed by this way and experienced life before us. It is said, "Youth is wasted on the young." I do not think so. I think that the young just have not had the great fortune to experience all of life's greatest challenges and mysteries of those who came before us have.

Living in the now is a gift that we can tap into right now. Right Now!

Titus 2:12
New King James Version (NKJV)
12 teaching us that, denying ungodliness and worldly lusts, we should live soberly, righteously, and godly in the present age.

7

BELIEVE OUTSIDE OF YOURSELF IN SOMETHING OTHER THAN YOU

Find your path by believing in Jesus Christ and many of the great saints and follow it. Follow it with all of your heart and soul. When you have focused your belief in Jesus Christ, you take the focus off yourself and onto him. You spill out of your capsule and pour your troubles into Jesus Christ. You empty yourself. You hide yourself in God.

Matthew 11:30 says, *"For My Yoke is Easy and My Burden is Light"*: In other works, give it to God!

It is said that we are a spiritual beings having a human experience. Did you know that we all have troubles? Did you know that nowhere in the Bible does it say that you will not have troubles? It does say that there is hope and strength in God. Isaiah 41:10 says, *"fear not, for I am with you; be not dismayed, for I am your God; I will strengthen you, I will uphold you with my righteous right hand."*

There is encouragement from Jesus and all of the great saints that have passed before us. Their words, their actions, their ways can be encouragement to you to survive any giant that may be trying to slay you. Bathe your mind in their words of encouragement and see what a positive difference it will make in your life.

Genesis 15:6
New King James Version (NKJV)
[6] And he believed in the Lord, and He account it to him for righteousness.

8

IT IS NOT ABOUT YOU

Hard to believe, but the world revolves around the sun and not you. You are not the center of the universe. Yes, we live with ourselves 24 hours a day, seven days a week. However, so does everyone else. We all have the same exact 24 hours in a day with ourselves. So why do some people with similar problems have an optimistic outlook on life? It is because they know that IT IS NOT ABOUT THEM.

When you are having a bad day, when others have criticized you, when they have cut you off in traffic, when they have said offensive things to you, please understand that it is not about you in anyway. They are frustrated with their own situation and are releasing it on you. You are just in their path. If it is an immediate family member that abuses you, get out of their space, if possible. Walk away. They are the one with the issues, not you. It is not about you.

Once you give them the consent to hurt you, then you hurt yourself. In other words, do not give them consent and their arrows of hatred will not affect you. Eleanor Roosevelt once said very eloquently, *"no one can make you feel inferior without your consent."* Do not give them your consent.

---

1 Samuel 9:20
New King James Version (NKJV)
[20] But as for your donkeys that were lost three days ago, do not be anxious about them, for they have been found. And on whom *is* all the desire of Israel? *Is it* not you and on all your father's house?"

9

DEATH IS IRREVERSIBLE

A comedian once said, *"It is not how you die that matters, it is who you take with you."* You are taking yourself to a place of no return. You physically cannot walk back into this life. Furthermore, you are leaving behind those that need and love you. You may not know that, but it is a fact. Many people decide to leave this life to get back at someone or to show how hurt they felt while alive. You may not be able to express your feeling openly, so you decide to end your life as an act of revenge.

This only crushes those who truly love you and accomplishes nothing. You leave behind grieving children, brothers, sisters, parents, spouses, friends and co-workers. You are loved very much. Just because your emotions are telling you to end everything, does not mean that you should. You have a responsibility to others, the world and God.

It is not a decision that you can reverse or change once you make up your mind and commit the act of suicide. You are gone. The emotional carnage left behind is unspeakable. Imagine if both of your parents decided to end their lives prior to you being born. Your beautiful smile, your great laughter, your wonderful caring would never have existed. You deserve to live and we deserve to have the honor of having you with us.

Revelation 20:15
New King James Version (NKJV)
15 And anyone not found written in the Book of Life was cast into the lake of fire.

10

WE ARE ALL IN THE SAME BOAT

It may seem that celebrities, famous athletes and the wealthy have it better than us…but it is an illusion. There are study after study that conclude that money does not bring more happiness. William Shakespeare said, *"Fame is an empty purse."* There are many celebrities that have fame and then disgrace. I am saying that we all have troubles and we are all in the same boat.

Spend a week watching the church channel or a channel based on spirituality. You will hear preacher after preacher speak about how desperate our situations are and how sad our lives have become. Notice how many people are in the pews watching those preachers. There are thousands! There are thousands of souls looking for help and direction with their lives.

This poem should help to emphasize my point:

If you have food in your fridge, clothes on your back, a roof over your head and a place to sleep you are richer than 75% of the world. If you have money in the bank, your wallet, and some spare change you are among the top 8% of the world's wealthy.

If you woke up this morning with more health than illness, you are more blessed than the million people who will not survive this week. If you have never experienced the danger of battle, the agony of imprisonment or torture, or the horrible pangs of starvation you are luckier than 500 million people alive and suffering. If you can read this message, you are more fortunate than 3 billion people in the world that cannot read it at all.

> **Romans 3:20**
> **The Message (MSG)**
> [9-20] So where does that put us? Do we Jews get a better break than the others? Not really. Basically, all of us, whether insiders or outsiders, start out in identical conditions, which is to say that we all start out as sinners. Scripture leaves no doubt about it.

11

FORGIVE YOUR PAST

We all have a past. I repeat….we all have a past. If you live long enough, you accumulate your past day by day and sometime make the wrong choice. This is part of learning and growing.

No matter what you have done or how badly you perceive what you have done, forgive yourself. Give yourself a break and forgive.

I have a saying, "Yes, what you heard about me is true, but only a hundred times worse." It is a hundred times worse because we beat ourselves up hundreds of times well after our mistake has been buried in the past. You made the mistake; there it is, so move on. Your past is like the winds that blow past you, never to return.

A great thing that will help you is to write down a forgiveness letter to those that you have wronged. Write yourself a letter forgiving yourself for what you had done. Let us look at it this way. Even the great Moses had murdered an Egyptian before crossing the Red Sea into Midian. He was forgiven by God and was given the Ten Commandments which still exist to this day. How much worse could your past be?

---

1 John 1:9
New International Version (NIV)
[9] If we confess our sins, he is faithful and just and will forgive us our sins and purify us from all unrighteousness.

12

FORGET WHAT YOU DID AND MOVE ON

Mother Teresa said it is not enough to forgive, but forgetting is the next step. If you can forget what you did, then you can forgive yourself. Can you imagine having no recall of ever offending anyone?

If you have no memory of an action, then you have no sorrow or guilt feelings. Always try your best to say that you are sorry, repent and move on. Forget your past and stop rehearsing it in your mind.

I know this is easier said than done, but here are a few tools that may be helpful. Whenever a bad thought arises in your mind, replace it. Some people recite the rosary repeatedly. Others say a prayer. Do what you have to do, but change your thought pattern as soon as possible. Water the good seed, not the bad one. Remember, it is the seed that you water that will be the one that grows.

I am suggesting that if you replace a negative thought pattern with a predetermined saying, then that can wipe out the negative thought. Remember that an empty mind is truly a devil's playground. So fill your mind with a predetermined thought and it will help.

Genesis 27:45
New International Version (NIV)
45 When your brother is no longer angry with you and forgets what you did to him, I'll send word for you to come back from there. Why should I lose both of you in one day?

13

FORGIVE THE WRONG DONE TO YOU

We all experience offense and wrong things done to us by others. There are no exceptions to the rule. No matter what your story is regarding what someone else did to you, somebody can top your story.

How bad can an offense be if you are alive and reading this book right now? Hundreds of thousands of people have died from the anger and/or revenge done to them by others. By forgiving the other person that hurt you, you take the high road and clear the negative energy that surrounds you.

Blessing the person that wronged you puts the wrong back onto them and moves it off you forever. I have had some of the worst things said to me out of anger or hatred just for being me. I had to learn to forgive that person by blessing them for doing that to me. I looked at it as a learning experience.

At first, the sting of being betrayed or offended can hurt very badly. Once you get a hold of yourself, you have to forgive them and then bless the person. Things always do come back around.

Whatever someone does to another, it will come back to him or her in either the same form or another. You do not want to have any attachment to someone's negativity, so forgive him or her and bless him or her. Then move on!

Matthew 6:15
New International Version (NIV)
15 But if you do not forgive others their sins, your Father will not forgive your sins.

14

FORGIVE THE WRONG YOU DID TO OTHERS

We all have wronged others. Not one of us is innocent of doing wrong to another. This is something that we do either unknowingly or out of extenuating circumstances. Whether you know it or not, you are the one who beats up on yourself relentlessly and repeatedly. That is of course, if you have a conscience. You have to move on and forgive yourself.

Ask both God and the person you have wronged to forgive you and release it. Asking for God's forgiveness is easy – just ask. Asking the person you have wronged is difficult at best. If you are uncomfortable with face-to-face encounters, then write a personal letter. Mailing a hand written letter to another can transfer your guilt onto the paper and get if off your mind and out of your soul.

If you have done that, then you can move past your feelings of guilt. The shame or guilt attached to the wrong that you have done to another is moved out of your sphere.

As children we betray our friends, lie to parents, and give false witness about a sibling to cover our wrongdoing. As adults, if we do not learn our lessons, we do the exact same things and worse. Ask again for forgiveness and believe that you are forgiven,.

Leviticus 19:22
New International Version (NIV)
[15] With the ram of the guilt offering the priest is to make atonement for him before the LORD for the sin he has committed, and his sin will be forgiven.

15

EVERY SAINT HAS A PAST AND EVERY SINNER HAS A FUTURE

Both Saint Augustine and Oscar Wilde have been given credit for this saying: "Every Saint has a past and every sinner has a future". Regardless of who came up with this, it is ever so true. All of us have done something so embarrassing or so horrific that it could change our destiny and future if it ever gets out there. Sometimes, when it does get out there, it is often used to either shame us or knock us down. With fame and notoriety often comes disgrace.

The best thing to do is to own up to it and move on. Your past is the past. Our eyes are in the front of our head and not in the back, so as not to look back and only forward.

Often people unknowingly criticize others out of jealousy and envy. Do not fall victim to their smallness. It is when you are flying high that they will try to shoot you down. Just realize that the same ones that are criticizing you are also guilty of something in their past. They are just trying to shine a light on you and off themselves.

In the New Testament, Matthew 7:5, Jesus said, "You hypocrite, take the plank out of your own eye, and then you will see clearly to remove the speck from your brother's eye." (NIV) We are all sinners and we can all be saints. We just have to confront our past, repent and move on.

Acts 9:1-43
English Standard Version (ESV)
9 But Saul, still breathing threats and murder against the disciples of the Lord, went to the high priest2 and asked him for letters to the synagogues at Damascus, so that if he found any belongings to the Way, men or women, he might bring them bound to Jerusalem. 3 Now as he went on his way, he approached Damascus, and suddenly a light from heaven shone around him. 4 And falling to the ground he heard a voice saying to him, "Saul, Saul, why are you persecuting me?" 5 And he said, "Who are you, Lord?" And he said, "I am Jesus, whom you are persecuting".

16

YOU ARE LOVED

Yes, you are so loved. Those that deeply love you can also deeply hurt you. There are no exceptions! The more that you are loved, the more that you hurt. Do you remember when your parents held back something that you wanted so much that you cried? My wife and I have cried just as my daughters cry when we don't allow them to have something they want. Your parents did it for your own good and benefit. In the long term, it was because they deeply loved you.

If you are not getting what you want right now, it is because you are deeply loved by God. What if you wanted a shiny new sports car and got it right when you learned to drive? That very evening you go speeding away in your new car. You cruise out of control and then are killed in a car crash. This very thing has happened to someone I read about in the newspaper. They got what they wanted but lost their life. God wants to keep you here and so do others.

You must learn to look at not getting what you want now, as getting something better later down the road. If I got everything I wanted, I would most likely be dead or very lost and unhappy. You are loved and needed. Someone may have said something that hurt you or you may be sick with cancer as you read this. This is all because you are loved and being made into a better, more evolved person.

You are loved!

Romans 1:7
New International Version (NIV)
7 To all in Rome who are loved by God and called to be his holy people. Grace and peace to you God our Father and the Lord Jesus Christ.

17

YOU ARE A MIRACLE

Do you have any idea how many sperm it takes to make a baby? Answer: just one. However, thousands of sperm are sent to fertilize an egg and you are that one who made it! What a miracle!

You are that miracle. Even before you took your first breath of air, you were chosen. Miracles should never be thrown away. There is a reason that you were the one chosen sperm that made it into this life.

In less developed countries, people are struggling to hold onto their lives, not throw them away. Take a week and go to the poorest area near where you live. Visit a soup kitchen or a homeless shelter and then compare it to your life. It is said that most of the happiest people are those that have the least amount. It is because we always want, want and want more.

Just watch a reality television show about the lives of the rich. They are on television fighting with their family members and screaming at one another. Not happy, just spoiled.

We have to realize what a miracle it is to be alive and what a miracle it is just to breathe and hear our heart beat. Appreciate the small miracle in your life. You are a miracle, so do not throw away the gift.

Psalm 77:14
New International Version (NIV)
[14] You are the God who performs miracles, you display your power among the peoples.

18

YOU ARE NEVER ALONE

Whatever your story is, I can tell you or refer you to someone who has it worse than you. I know of a couple who lost their only daughter at 7 years of age to an inoperable brain tumor. I really cannot imagine the pain of losing a child at any age. Just realize that life is fragile. No one of us has immunity from life's pains and the possibility of a catastrophe happening to us at any moment.

However, just as things can change for the worse in the blink of an eye, they too can change for the better in the blink of an eye. When feeling poor, poor me, and God, why me…just go to a children's hospital and visit the cancer ward. Also, visit a large city in your vicinity and see the homeless shivering along the cold, hard sidewalk asking for your money. I have had the honor of visiting China on two occasions. Both times, I saw the poorest of poor. It is a wakeup call that your life is not so bad.

I remember feeling so low when someone I loved very much and was in a relationship with for eight years, left me for someone else. I then found out later that the girl I was in love with had been unfaithful to me for many years with my friend. I had to practice forgiveness in a big way. Today I thank God that the relationship had ended when it did. Today, I have a beautiful wife and two beautiful children. At that point in time during my break-up, I could not see the great future that God had in store for me down the road. Remember, you are never alone!

Numbers 11:17
New International Version (NIV)
[17] I will come down and speak with you there, and I will take some of the power of the Spirit that is on you and put it on them. They will share the burden of the people with you so that you will not have to carry it alone.

19

PAIN MAKES YOU STRONGER

I have heard that what does not kill you makes you stronger. I would like to add, wiser too. Can you remember a time in your life that you thought you would not make it through a situation? Maybe you were scheduled to fight a bully on your school bus after school. Maybe you were diagnosed with a form of cancer. If you hang in there however, you can get through to the other end no matter what the outcome. When you get out from that dark tunnel, you really do become stronger and wiser.

You became stronger and wiser because you chose to stay and stick it out. You learned not to run from the situation. When dealing with incredible pain, let it pass through you. It has to pass through or it will manifest itself into something much worse. A small tumor ignored or not treated properly grows into a larger tumor that you have to eventually deal with. Deal with the pain now and get through it.

It is said that a man's son was killed in battle. That evening the father went out dancing at a party. While at a party, a woman asked him how he could be out dancing when his son was just killed in battle. The man replied, "If I do not get over it now, it will kill me later."

---

1 Peter 4:11
Whoever speaks, as one who speaks oracles of God; whoever serves, as one who serves by the strength that God supplies – in order that in everything God may be glorified through Jesus Christ. To him belong glory and dominion forever and ever. Amen.

20

PRAY AND MEDITATE

Praying can change anything in the blink of an eye. Your life can change for the better immediately with a prayer from the heart. I remember one time when I was so distraught over a particular situation, I prayed so hard that afternoon and by that evening, the situation went away.

Prayer is proven to lower your blood pressure and can have many of the same affects as effective exercise. You are seeking divine guidance for something that is perceived as the impossible to you. This world is a physical world only. There is a supernatural world that is accessible when we concentrate on God and move out of our own person. We truly are spiritual beings having a human experience.

No matter how bad or irreversible your situation seems, pray. It will change everything. This simple prayer has worked wonders for me "Lord, Jesus Christ, son of God, please have mercy on me a sinner". This prayer is better known in Europe as the Jesus Prayer. For whatever reason, the Jesus prayer is not as popular in the west or in North America.

The rosary is a great source of inspiration to. There is overwhelming research to prove its power to change anything for those who believe. That is the key, the entire key. Believe and have faith.

Genesis 24:12
New International Version (NIV)
[12] Then he prayed, "Lord, God of my master Abraham, make me successful today, and show kindness to my master Abraham.

21

THOSE WHO HAVE OVERCOME

There are many others that have been through the hardest times imaginable and come out the other side. Here are just a few names of those that have survived unspeakable pain and suffering and have lived to tell their story.

Immaculee Ilibagiza is a Rwandan genocide survivor. Immaculee was concealed in a 3-foot by 4-foot bathroom with seven other women for 91 days. While Immaculee was concealed, she was being hunted the entire time.

Viktor Fankl spent three years in a Nazi concentration camp.. Viktor lost his wife, mother and brother in the Nazi concentration camps while he survived. After his release in 1945, he wrote the book entitled, <u>Trotzdem Ja Zum Leven Sagen: Ein Psychologe Erlebt das Konzentrationslager</u> (translated: "...Saying Yes to Life in Spite of Everything: A Psychologist Experiences the Concentration Camp", know in English by the title <u>Man's Search for Meaning</u>, 1995.

Tsutomu Yamaguchi survived the atomic bomb dropped on Hiroshima and Nagasaki in 1945. When he did die, he died of stomach cancer at the age of 93.

These people survived the most astonishing odds against them. They all are reported as having seen their lives as a blessing even after such horrific experiences.

New International Version (2011)
"I have told you these things, so that in me you may have peace. In this world you have trouble. But take heart! I have overcome the world."

22

LOOK TO THE FUTURE

Your future is at your doorstep. Your future is the next second and moment in front of you. Right now, your life is changing for the best. Yes! Right now, you can choose to be happy or unhappy. The choice to be happy is the best path. Happiness is like an education, it cannot be taken away from you. You were once happy, so why not put yourself back there? Adding one minute of unhappiness or depression to your circumstances will not change one thing.

Happiness is a frame of mind. Framing a piece of art can be as much of the art as the art itself. You look at the whole art hanging on the wall. Now look to the future with the whole you surrounded by happiness. It really is a choice.

The Dalai Lama said, "Happiness is not something readymade. It comes from your own actions." You have a great future no matter where you are or what your plight in life may be. If you are in prison for 20+ years, maybe in the next appeal process, your sentence will be reduced for good behavior.

Your past does not dictate your future. If you were abused by a spouse or given false testimony against, then that is gone in the wind. Move forward and do not rehearse your past life. That was yesterday. Tomorrow does not have to be a mystery if you go into it with a great attitude of happiness.

Isaiah 43:18-19
"Forget the former things;
do not dwell on the past.
See, I am doing a new thing!
Now it springs up; do you not perceive it?
I am making a way in the desert and streams in the wasteland." (NIV)

23

LOVE YOURSELF FOR WHO YOU ARE

Why beat yourself up? You are made perfectly and that includes warts and all. Why is it so hard to forgive yourself? Getting past your past is something that we all need to do. You are beautifully made and crafted. There is no other you. No other person has your hands, eyes, hair, color, feet, and the body that you possess. How beautifully you truly are, just as you are right now.

There will always be others that will not like you. It is because they do not like themselves or see something in you that they do not like in themselves.

Eleanor Roosevelt said, "No one can make you feel inferior without your consent." If someone cannot have the tallest building in town, then they tear down all the tall buildings so their building will be the tallest. So do not tear yourself down. Do not beat yourself up over and over again. Let go. Stop wrestling with yourself. Get a hold of your emotions and get a grip on yourself.

You must realize that you are not perfect and no one else is either. Love yourself because you have to live with yourself 24 hours, 7 days a week. You cannot control others or their actions. So do not accept their insults or violent actions toward you. Do not let them steal your joy. You can control the joy you have by not letting them steal it from you. The Beatles said, "All you need is love."

---

1 John 3:1
See what kind of love the Father has given to us, that we should be called children of God; and so we are. The reason why the world does not know us is that it did not know him.

24

VISUALIZE GREATNESS AND CHANGE

I read a story where a woman in Los Angeles, California was totally broke. In addition, she was raising her sister's four children as her sister had just passed away. This woman visualized winning the million dollar lottery. She visualized the shirt that she would be wearing on the day she won. Well, as the story goes, she did win the million dollar lottery months later after visualizing it. Also, she was wearing the shirt that she visualized she would wear that same day!

Just as this woman had done, so be it unto you. You can visualize the change that you want to be. Sit quietly for a few minutes each day and think about the person that you want to become or the change in your life that you are wishing for. Visualize the colors, the scents and the scenery of the surrounding in your very best future and it will be. Do not think about your current circumstances. Just look to the change. Of course, you still will have to put in the time and work involved to make this change happen.....just work towards it.

Many of those that have become successful in their lives have come from humble and poor beginnings. The difference was that they saw a better future for themselves and became that future that they predicted. This visualization can work in the reverse as well. If you are always complaining or thinking about when the other shoe will fall, then you will put yourself on that path. So think about the positive change that you want for yourself and you will become that change. You will of course make this a better world in the process.

Philippians 4:13 ESV
I can do all things through him who strengthens me.

25

WHERE TO GO FROM HERE

The very first thing is to reconsider your life and all that your are worth. God has great plans for you and wants you to be as great as you can be. Regardless of your current situation, you can change your outlook and move into a better perspective on your life. Everything is very temporary, our lives, our natural state of being. Please stop trying to be the one to change your destiny. Put everything in God's hands and all will work out for the best.

Yes, bad things do happen to good people and you are truly never alone. There are support groups on-line to go to. You can call the Nation Suicide Prevention Lifeline at 1-800-237-TALK (8255). They are available on-line at www.suicidepreventionlifeline.org.

They are there to assist and help you. Nobody truly wants to die. Nobody wants you to die! It does not matter what has happened to you, you are here for a reason. So, please be that reason to survive the odds and live the life that God has intended for you. Remember, there is always tomorrow. There is always hope.

Job 17:9
"The righteous keep moving forward, and those with clean hands become stronger and stronger." (NLT)

26

EPILOGUE

This book is written for those that have thoughts of suicide.

This book does not in any way replace or cancel out the use of professional help or prescribed medications for those with psychological conditions. Nor does this book take the place of professional help or prescribed medications for anyone with severe depression of any kind.

This book is to be read and practiced in addition to the above mentioned.

Please know that you are always loved by God.

God Bless you!

ABOUT THE AUTHOR

Bob Miles lives in Pennsylvania with his wife Janet and their two daughters Lily and Chloe.

Bob had a popular cable television show "Miles of Music". www.milesofmusic.tv

Bob also has the website www.saytherosary.org.

Bob's other books, Ego – Entering God's Oneness, 25 Ways to Let Go of Your Ego and 25 Great Joys You Will Experience Once You Adopt a Child are available on-line.